GIVE UP AND LOSE THE GAME

A Dynamic Journey of Learning, Growth, and Endless Possibility

Copyright

Table of contents

INTRODUCTION:

Are you ready to embark on a journey to uncover the mystery of success? It's a quest that we all pursue throughout our lives, but what is success, if not a subjective and ever-changing concept? To understand it, we must think of life as a game board, with each decision and action propelling us forward. Success is the ultimate goal, but unlike traditional board games, the rules of this game are only limited by our imagination and perseverance.

Winning and losing become integral components of this metaphorical gameplay. We must maneuver through a maze of challenges, with victories serving as level completions and setbacks akin to temporary defeats. Winning doesn't mean the absence of obstacles, but rather the mastery of overcoming them. It's about accumulating experiences, skills, and achievements as we progress through different levels. Losing is not a permanent state, but a momentary setback—a chance to learn, adapt, and become stronger.

We are the players in this game of success, and we hold the controller of our destinies. The decisions we make, the alliances we form, and the challenges we confront all contribute to our unique gameplay. The journey is unpredictable, and the outcome is uncertain, but that's the beauty of the game—its unpredictability, its capacity to surprise and inspire.

Let's explore the rules, strategies, and hidden levels that define this extraordinary game of life. Together, we'll uncover the secrets of the ultimate game—success.

My Journey*

As the sun set, I found myself standing at a
crossroads, faced with a decision that could alter
the course of my life. It was a moment that
reminded me of a high-stakes game, where the
consequences of failure were real.

A few years ago, I was stuck in a mundane job
that brought me no joy. Every day felt like a
repeat of the last, and I felt like I was being dealt
a bad hand. But then, I heard a whisper of
possibility, a dream that seemed to call to me
from the depths of my soul.

This dream was different from anything I had
ever known, and it scared me. But it also
promised potential, and I knew that staying in
my current situation was a riskier game. So, I
decided to take a leap of faith and pursue my
dream.

This decision changed my life. It was the first move in a game where giving up meant losing the very thing I was striving for.

Come with me on a journey through this book, as I explore the highs and lows of success. Let my story be a reminder of the power of embracing the unknown and chasing after our dreams.

Chapter 1: The Rules of the Game

In the grand arena of success, there is an unspoken code - a set of rules that govern the rise and fall of this complex game. These rules, much like the laws of physics, shape the dynamics of our journey and influence the results we strive to achieve. As we embark on this exploration, let's decipher the fundamental principles that define the game of success.

Rule 1: Clarity of Goals
Success starts with a clear understanding of one's objectives. Just as a skilled player navigates a game with a specific mission, those seeking success must articulate their goals. The clarity of purpose acts as a compass, guiding decisions and actions in line with the ultimate quest.

Rule 2: Strategy and Planning

Every game requires a strategy - a roadmap that outlines the path from beginning to victory. Success also requires careful planning. Explore the details of your objectives, anticipate challenges, and create a flexible strategy that can accommodate the unpredictable turns of the journey.

Rule 3: Persistence in the Face of Challenges
If there is one constant in the game of success, it is the inevitability of challenges. Persistence, the tenacity to endure setbacks and persist in the face of adversity, is a non-negotiable rule. Much like a seasoned gamer attempts a difficult level multiple times, success favors those who keep going, learning and adapting with each encounter.

Anecdote: The Marathon of Persistence

Let me share a personal story that highlights the importance of persistence. In my early ventures, success seemed like an unattainable dream.

Rejections, failures, and unexpected obstacles were constant companions. However, it was during these moments of trial that I discovered the game-changing power of persistence. Each setback, rather than a sign to give up, became a stepping stone to resilience. The marathon of persistence made the journey itself a victory, proving that in the game of success, endurance is a game-changer.

Rule 4: Adaptability and Agility
In this dynamic game, adaptability is a defining rule. Much like a player adjusting their strategy to unexpected in-game events, those seeking success must embrace change. Agility in thought and action allows one to navigate the ever-changing landscape with finesse, turning challenges into opportunities.

Rule 5: Learning from Setbacks
Failure, often seen as the opposite of success, is an essential part of the game. The rule here is not to avoid failure but to use it as a powerful tool for learning. Each misstep reveals valuable

insights, shaping a player's growth. Success, therefore, is not just about avoiding defeat but about growing through it.

** Key Players and Influencers**

Success is not a solo mission, it's a multiplayer experience. As we embark on this journey, let's take a look at the key players and influencers who play a major role in the game of success.

Player 1: Mentor, the Guide
The Mentor is a seasoned player who has already gone through the levels we are yet to face. Their wisdom and experience become a beacon of light in our journey. They provide us with knowledge and invaluable insights, helping us to tackle obstacles with a more nuanced approach. From career advice to life lessons, the Mentor is a catalyst for growth and resilience.

Player 2: Ally, the Co-op Companion
Success is often a team effort, and the Ally is a trusted companion in this multiplayer game. Whether in the professional world or personal pursuits, Allies offer support, encouragement, and shared victories. Their presence turns challenges into shared experiences, making the

journey more enjoyable. In the game of success, forming strong alliances is not only a strategy but also a key to unlocking higher levels of achievement.

Player 3: Adversity, the Challenger
No game is complete without its challenges, and in the game of success, Adversity plays a crucial role. While initially seen as a formidable opponent, Adversity is actually a key player that tests our skills, resilience, and determination. By embracing these challenges as opportunities for growth, we learn to navigate the complexities of the game and become stronger with each encounter.

Player 4: Innovation, the Game-Changer
Innovation is the disruptor, the player who introduces new strategies, ideas, and perspectives to the game. Much like unlocking a powerful weapon or ability in a game, embracing innovation propels us forward, giving us a competitive edge. This player challenges the status quo, encourages creativity, and opens

doors to unexplored territories within the game
of success.

Anecdote: The Mentor's Wisdom

I'd like to share a personal experience with the
Mentor player. During a crucial phase in my
career, I found myself at a crossroads, not
knowing what to do next. A mentor, with years
of experience in the industry, provided me with
invaluable guidance. Their insights not only
cleared my path but also gave me a sense of
confidence. This encounter highlighted the
importance of key players in the game, showing
how the wisdom of a mentor can be the
game-changing move needed to overcome a
difficult level.

Chapter 2: Choosing Your Team

Assembling the right team is a key part of the game of success. Your team of allies, mentors, and influencers can make or break your progress, so it's important to choose wisely. Allies are your comrades, offering support and encouragement. Mentors are experienced players who can provide invaluable advice and guidance. Influencers are game-changers who bring fresh perspectives and innovative ideas.

I can personally attest to the power of allies. During a difficult project, my allies keep morale high and fostered collaboration. Their support made all the difference, and it goes to show how much of an impact the right team can have.

Selecting your team is an active strategy that requires careful thought. Make sure to choose individuals who align with your values and goals, and who will contribute to your ultimate success.

Stories of Triumph and Support Systems

Success stories are not just about one person, but rather a collective effort of many people who have come together to help an individual reach their goals. In this chapter, we explore the inspiring tales of those who have achieved success, and the profound impact their support systems had on their journey.

Take the example of Steve Jobs, the co-founder of Apple Inc. His adoptive father, Paul Jobs, was a major influence in his life. Paul, a mechanic and carpenter, not only encouraged Steve's interest in electronics, but also instilled in him a passion for craftsmanship. This mentorship, rooted in familial bonds, was a key factor in Steve Jobs' innovative spirit. Paul's guidance and unwavering support was instrumental in the success of one of the most influential figures in the tech industry.

Another example is the partnership between Bill Gates and Paul Allen, the co-founders of

Microsoft. Their shared vision, complementary skills, and mutual support enabled them to turn a garage project into a global powerhouse. This alliance between Gates and Allen is a testament to the power of allies, and how they can help an individual reach their goals.

The friendship between Oprah Winfrey and Maya Angelou is another example of how influencers can shape perspectives. Oprah credits much of her success to the guidance and wisdom of Maya Angelou, a renowned author and poet. Angelou's influence extended beyond professional advice; she became a mentor, friend, and source of inspiration. This synergy between these two influential figures highlights the profound impact influencers can have on shaping not just careers but also personal growth and resilience.

These stories demonstrate that success is not a solitary journey. It's a collaborative effort, a symphony of relationships that amplify individual capabilities. From my own experiences, I can attest to the transformative power of mentors, allies, and influencers. Success, in its truest form, is a shared victory.

Chapter 3: Levels and Challenges

Success is like a complex game with different levels, each with its own set of challenges and opportunities. In this chapter, we will explore the concept of success by breaking it down into levels and examining the obstacles that come with each stage.

1. Level 1: Clarity and Vision

The first level of success is all about gaining clarity and defining your vision. Think of this as the tutorial phase, where you learn the basics of the game. Challenges at this stage usually involve self-reflection, setting clear objectives, and understanding your motivations. Overcoming these challenges will open the door to the next levels, laying the groundwork for the journey ahead.

2. Level 2: Strategy and Planning

As you move forward, success requires strategic thinking and careful planning. This level is like a puzzle, where you have to put the pieces of your goals together and create a roadmap. Challenges here may include dealing with uncertainties, making tough decisions, and refining your strategies. Successfully overcoming these challenges will take you further into the game, with a well-thought-out plan.

3. Level 3: Persistence Amidst Adversity

Success, like a difficult boss battle, often tests your resilience and determination. This level brings adversities—unexpected setbacks, failures, and obstacles that require persistence to overcome. Navigating this stage involves developing a mindset that sees setbacks not as defeats but as opportunities for growth. Each conquered challenge becomes a stepping stone to greater accomplishments.

Anecdote: The Uncharted Levels

In my own journey, Level 3 was a crucial phase. When I faced unexpected setbacks, I initially saw them as insurmountable roadblocks. However, adopting a gamer's mindset—viewing challenges as chances to level up—changed my approach. Each adversity became a chance to hone my skills and refine my strategies, showing the transformative power of navigating the uncharted levels of success.

4. Level 4: Skill Development and Mastery

Just like characters in a game acquire new skills to progress, success requires continuous skill development. This level involves honing your abilities, gaining new knowledge, and mastering the tools necessary for your journey. Challenges here involve leaving your comfort zone, embracing a growth mindset, and committing to lifelong learning.

5. Level 5: Resilience in the Endgame

The last levels of success often involve a combination of skills, experiences, and challenges. This endgame phase may bring its own unique set of trials—perhaps dealing with the pressures of success, managing newfound responsibilities, or redefining goals. Resilience is the key factor here, ensuring that you not only reach the peak of success but also sustain and thrive in the aftermath.

** Embracing Failure: A Temporary Setback
and a Learning Opportunity**

Playing the game of success is not a straight path
to victory, but rather a journey with its own set
of challenges. Failure is an integral part of this
journey, and it can be seen as a dynamic
element—a temporary setback that can provide
invaluable lessons and opportunities for growth.
This chapter will explore the power of viewing
failure through the lens of resilience, and how it
can be used as a pivotal phase in the quest for
success.

The idea of a game where every move and
decision leads to immediate success may sound
appealing, but it would lack the challenge, the
thrill of overcoming obstacles, and the
satisfaction of leveling up. Failure is the player's
manual, guiding us through the intricacies of the
journey.

Rather than seeing failure as a daunting abyss, it
is important to recognize it as a temporary

setback—a momentary pause in the gameplay. Just as a character in a game respawns after falling, individuals experiencing setbacks have the opportunity to regroup, reassess, and re-enter the game with newfound insights. Success, in its truest form, is the result of navigating through these setbacks with resilience and perseverance.

Take the example of J.K. Rowling, author of the immensely successful Harry Potter series. Before achieving literary stardom, Rowling faced numerous rejections from publishers. Instead of succumbing to the setbacks, she embraced failure as a temporary setback, using it as fuel to refine her craft. Rowling's resilience transformed her into a literary phoenix, rising from the ashes of rejection to become one of the most celebrated authors in the world.

Failure is not just a pause button but a treasure trove of learning opportunities. Each misstep, every wrong turn in the game of success, reveals insights that guide future strategies. The ability to extract lessons from failure is a skill that distinguishes successful players in the journey of life. It's about asking the right questions, analyzing the gameplay, and using failure as a springboard for improvement.

The fear of failure can be a formidable adversary, paralyzing individuals and hindering progress. However, once we recognize failure as a natural part of the game, the fear loses its grip. Instead of dreading failure, we can approach it with a gamer's mindset—ready to learn, adapt, and respawn stronger.

Resilience, the ability to bounce back from setbacks, is a critical skill in the game of success. Failure, when embraced with resilience, becomes a catalyst for personal and professional growth. Each failure becomes a checkpoint, marking progress and reinforcing the player's capacity to endure, learn, and ultimately triumph.

triumph over adversity: personal stories of resilience

The intricate narrative of success is often characterized by triumph emerging from the crucible of adversity. This chapter is devoted to personal stories and case studies that demonstrate the resilience, determination, and unwavering spirit of individuals who have overcome formidable obstacles in their pursuit of success.

1. The Rocky Ascent: Sylvester Stallone's Unwavering Spirit

Sylvester Stallone's journey to stardom is a tale of relentless perseverance. Before becoming the iconic Rocky Balboa, Stallone encountered numerous rejections and financial difficulties. In a pivotal moment of adversity, he chose to write the screenplay for "Rocky" himself, a film that would eventually become a cinematic phenomenon. Stallone's story is a testament to the power of resilience and the transformative potential of challenges.

2. Rising from the Ashes: J.K. Rowling's Literary Odyssey

J.K. Rowling, celebrated author of the Harry Potter series, faced her fair share of challenges before achieving literary acclaim. From battling financial hardship as a single mother to facing rejection from multiple publishers, Rowling's story is a reminder of the power of unwavering determination. It was in the face of adversity that she discovered the depth of her creativity and resilience, ultimately crafting a world that captivated millions.

Case Study: The Silicon Valley Visionary - Elon Musk

Elon Musk, the visionary entrepreneur behind companies like Tesla and SpaceX, encountered numerous setbacks on his path to success. From financial troubles to technical challenges, Musk's ventures were constantly under scrutiny. However, his ability to view setbacks as learning opportunities enabled him to iterate, innovate, and eventually redefine industries. Musk's story is a reminder of the transformative potential of resilience and a commitment to learning from challenges.

3. The Power of Inner Strength: Malala Yousafzai's Courageous Journey

Malala Yousafzai's story is a testament to the transformative power of inner strength. After surviving a Taliban attack for advocating girls' education, Malala emerged not only as a symbol of resilience but also as a global advocate for education and women's rights. Her unwavering commitment to her cause, even in the face of adversity, exemplifies the profound impact an individual can have when fueled by resilience and purpose.

4. A Musical Resurgence: The Phoenix of Robert Downey Jr.

Robert Downey Jr.'s journey from personal struggles to becoming one of Hollywood's highest-paid actors is a story of redemption. Overcoming legal issues and substance abuse, Downey Jr. rebuilt his career through sheer determination. His resurgence as Iron Man in the Marvel Cinematic Universe is a reminder of the transformative power of overcoming personal challenges and embracing a path of recovery.

Chapter 4: The Power of Strategy

In the complex game of success, strategy is the driving force that turns dreams into tangible accomplishments. This chapter is devoted to exploring the critical importance of strategy—a dynamic plan that guides decisions, overcomes obstacles, and helps individuals reach their goals in the great game of success.

1. Knowing the Game Board: Clarity of Objectives

In any game, understanding the rules and objectives is essential. Strategy in the game of success starts with gaining clarity on personal and professional objectives. This requires a thorough self-assessment to identify aspirations, strengths, and areas for improvement. Much like a skilled player studying the game board, this step sets the groundwork for strategic decision-making.

2. Plotting the Course: Crafting a Roadmap

A strategic roadmap is like planning moves in advance. It involves mapping out short-term and long-term goals, recognizing potential challenges, and creating a step-by-step plan to navigate the journey. Just as a player anticipates obstacles in a game, strategic planning allows individuals to prepare for potential roadblocks and adjust their approach accordingly.

Anecdote: The Chessboard of Entrepreneurship

Take the story of a budding entrepreneur who set out on the journey of starting a business. Faced with uncertainties and market difficulties, they created a strategic business plan—a chessboard of moves that considered market trends, competition, and potential risks. The strategic approach not only helped them get through initial challenges but also provided a framework for adapting to the ever-changing dynamics of the business world.

3. Maneuvering Through Levels: Adaptability and Agility

In the dynamic game of success, adaptability is a key part of effective strategy. Strategies that work are not rigid but flexible, able to evolve with changing circumstances. Successful players recognize the need to maneuver through different levels, adjusting their strategies based on new information, opportunities, and challenges.

4. Utilizing Power-Ups: Recognizing and Seizing Opportunities

Just like a gamer looks for power-ups for enhanced abilities, strategic individuals recognize and take advantage of opportunities for growth. A major part of strategic thinking is the ability to identify potential advantages, whether in the form of emerging trends, networking possibilities, or innovative ideas. The strategic player views opportunities not as random occurrences but as strategic moves that can boost their gameplay.

5. The Art of Resource Allocation: Efficient Decision-Making

Strategic decision-making involves carefully allocating resources—time, energy, and capital. Whether in personal or professional endeavors, understanding how to prioritize tasks and allocate resources efficiently is a critical aspect of strategic thinking. This skill enables players in the game of success to optimize their efforts, ensuring maximum impact.

Navigating Success: Exploring Strategies for Achievement

In the ever-changing game of success, there is no one-size-fits-all approach to achieving goals. This chapter is dedicated to exploring a variety of strategies that individuals can customize to their own personalities, preferences, and objectives. Let's embark on a journey to uncover the strategies that will help you reach your success goals.

1. The Incremental Approach: Small Steps Lead to Big Victories

The incremental approach is a strategy that involves breaking down large goals into smaller, achievable tasks and celebrating each accomplishment. This method emphasizes the power of consistent progress, much like leveling up in a game. By taking small steps, you can gradually build momentum and eventually reach your goals.

2. The Vision Board: Visualization and Attraction

The strategy of the vision board is a powerful tool for those who find strength in visualization. Creating a visual representation of your goals and aspirations helps you stay focused on your objectives and serves as a constant reminder of your destination. It also helps to attract the energy needed for success.

Anecdote: The Vision Board's Manifestation

A professional athlete used the strategy of a vision board to manifest success. They crafted a visual representation of their goals—images of podiums, medals, and triumphant moments—which fueled their motivation and served as a source of inspiration during challenging times. In the end, the athlete stood on the podium, realizing the goals that had once adorned their vision board.

3. Time Blocking: Efficient Time Management

Time blocking is a strategy that involves allocating specific time slots for different tasks and priorities. This approach helps you optimize your time and dedicate your focus to key activities. By organizing your day into distinct blocks, you can enhance your productivity and make meaningful strides toward your goals.

4. The Network Effect: Collaborative Achievement

The strategy of the network effect emphasizes the power of alliances and partnerships. Building a strong professional and personal network creates a support system that can help you reach your goals. Collaborative strategies involve leveraging the strengths of your network, whether through mentorship, joint ventures, or shared resources.

Read my book: **The Success You Can't See:**

Unlock the potential of 21 Digital Skills To Earn Money Before the Year Ends

5. The 80/20 Principle: Focusing on High-Impact Activities

The 80/20 principle, also known as the Pareto Principle, is a strategy that involves identifying the 20% of activities that yield 80% of the results. This approach emphasizes focusing on high-impact tasks that contribute significantly to goal achievement. By prioritizing key activities, you can optimize your efforts and streamline your path to success.

6. The Experimentation Mindset: Learning Through Iteration

The strategy of the experimentation mindset involves viewing goals as hypotheses to be tested and refined. This approach encourages you to iterate, learn from failures, and adapt your approaches based on real-time feedback. This mindset values the learning process as a critical component of success.

Chapter 5: The Art of Adaptability: Changing Strategies in the Game of Success

Success is a journey, not a destination, and adaptability is the superpower that allows individuals to navigate the ever-changing landscape with finesse. This chapter explores the importance of being able to adjust strategies when needed and how this skill can be a game-changer on the path to success.

Recognizing the dynamic nature of the game is the first step to embracing adaptability. Circumstances can change, unexpected challenges can arise, and external factors can shift, so successful players understand that their strategies must evolve with the environment. Pivoting, or changing course when necessary, is a strategic move that demonstrates adaptability.

Knowing when to hold onto a strategy and when to let it go is key to navigating the game.

Adaptability is also closely linked to the ability to learn from setbacks. When faced with challenges, successful players don't just endure, they learn, adapt, and recalibrate their strategies. Setbacks become powerful lessons that inform strategic adjustments and equip individuals for future levels of the game.

Innovation is a natural ally of adaptability. Successful players recognize that innovation often requires a departure from conventional strategies. Embracing new ideas, technologies, and approaches is a strategic revolution that allows individuals to stay ahead of the curve.

Dynamic decision-making is another hallmark of adaptability. Rather than relying on a rigid plan, successful individuals adjust their strategies based on the unfolding circumstances. This nimble approach ensures that decisions align with current realities and optimize the chances of success.

Finally, having a versatile toolkit of strategies is essential for adaptability. Instead of relying on a single, rigid approach, successful players cultivate a range of strategies that can be deployed based on the specific challenges and opportunities they encounter. This versatility ensures that they are well-equipped to navigate the diverse levels and scenarios in the game of success.

Mastering the Skill Tree: The Significance of Skill Development in the Journey to Success

Success is a complex game, and the skill tree is a hierarchical structure of interconnected abilities and competencies that can help players reach their goals. Developing and refining skills is a dynamic force that can propel individuals towards triumph in the multifaceted game of life. It is an ongoing, iterative process that requires a commitment to lifelong learning and an openness to acquiring new skills as the game evolves.

To strategically acquire skills, players must align their development efforts with their objectives. It is also important to stay agile and adapt to skill evolution by recognizing industry trends, technological advancements, and changing demands. Soft skills, such as interpersonal, communication, and emotional intelligence, are the power-ups of success and can help differentiate exceptional players. Finally, leveraging interconnected skills can create a

powerful network of competencies that
contribute to success.

The Skill Tree: Navigating Abilities for Success

Success can be thought of as a complex game, and the Skill Tree is a dynamic framework that serves as a blueprint for personal and professional growth. This metaphorical Skill Tree is a hierarchical structure with various branches, each representing a unique set of abilities and competencies. Let's take a look at the different branches of the Skill Tree and how they contribute to the mastery needed to succeed in life.

1. Technical Proficiency: The Foundation Branch

At the base of the Skill Tree is the Foundation Branch—Technical Proficiency. This includes specialized knowledge and skills that are relevant to your field of expertise. Whether it's coding for a software developer, engineering skills for an architect, or analytical skills for a data scientist, technical proficiency forms the solid foundation on which the rest of the Skill Tree can be built.

2. Communication Skills: The Networking Branch

The Networking Branch branches out from the foundation and represents the ability to communicate effectively. This includes not only verbal and written communication but also active listening—a skill that is often underestimated. A strong networking branch can enhance collaboration, foster healthy relationships, and open doors to opportunities in the game of success.

3. Leadership Abilities: The Growth Branch

The Growth Branch is located higher up in the Skill Tree and signifies leadership abilities. This branch is essential for those who aspire to lead teams or initiatives. Leadership involves not only directing others but also inspiring and empowering them to reach their full potential.

The Growth Branch allows individuals to navigate challenges, foster innovation, and create a positive impact on their surroundings.

4. Emotional Intelligence: The Adaptability Branch

The Adaptability Branch is located in a higher tier of the Skill Tree and represents emotional intelligence. This involves self-awareness, empathy, and the ability to navigate complex social dynamics. Like a resilient branch that sways with the winds of change, emotional intelligence enables individuals to adapt to diverse environments, manage stress, and build strong, meaningful connections.

5. Problem-Solving Skills: The Innovation Branch

The Innovation Branch symbolizes problem-solving skills, which are essential for overcoming obstacles and seizing opportunities. This branch encourages individuals to approach challenges with creativity, critical thinking, and a solutions-oriented mindset. Those who master the Innovation Branch can navigate complex problems with agility, contributing to their overall success in the game.

6. Time Management: The Efficiency Branch

The Efficiency Branch is located higher up in the Skill Tree and represents time management skills. Success often depends on how effectively one allocates and utilizes their time. The Efficiency Branch ensures that players in the game of success optimize their efforts, prioritize tasks, and maintain a balance between personal and professional commitments.

7. Resilience: The Endurance Branch

At the pinnacle of the Skill Tree is the Endurance Branch—symbolizing resilience. This branch equips individuals with the ability to bounce back from setbacks, learn from failures,

and persevere in the face of challenges.
Mastering the Endurance Branch ensures that
players not only reach the pinnacle of success
but also sustain their achievements over time.

Just like in a game where leveling up in one
branch unlocks new abilities, mastering different
branches of the Skill Tree provides individuals
with a comprehensive set of competencies.

The Path to Mastery: Practical Tips for Continuous Learning and Skill Enhancement

In the ever-changing game of success, the path to mastery is an ongoing quest for growth and improvement. This chapter is devoted to providing useful advice for ongoing learning and skill development—a roadmap for those looking to upgrade their abilities and tackle the ever-evolving challenges of the game.

1. Foster a Growth Mindset

The basis of continuous learning is fostering a growth mindset. Embrace difficulties as chances for growth, view effort as the way to mastery, and learn from criticism as constructive feedback. A growth mindset opens the door to continuous progress, allowing players to approach each level of the game with enthusiasm and resilience.

2. Establish Clear Learning Objectives

Clearly define your learning objectives. Whether it's gaining a new technical skill, improving leadership abilities, or honing time management, having specific goals gives direction to your learning journey. Break down larger objectives into smaller, achievable goals to track your progress effectively.

3. Utilize Online Learning Platforms

Take advantage of the abundance of online learning platforms. Platforms like Coursera, LinkedIn Learning, and Udemy offer a wide range of courses covering various skills and industries. These platforms provide flexibility, allowing players to learn at their own pace and tailor their learning experiences to align with their goals.

4. Participate in Workshops and Seminars

Engage in workshops, seminars, and industry events. These platforms offer chances to learn from experts, network with peers, and gain insights into the latest trends and advancements. Active participation in such events can broaden your perspective and expose you to new ideas and methodologies.

5. Seek Feedback and Mentorship

Feedback is a valuable tool for improvement. Actively seek feedback from peers, mentors, or supervisors to gain insights into your strengths and areas for development. Establishing mentorship relationships can provide personalized guidance, offering a unique perspective on skill enhancement tailored to your specific goals.

6. Create a Learning Schedule

Incorporate learning into your daily or weekly schedule. Allocate dedicated time for continuous learning, treating it as a non-negotiable commitment. Consistency is key, and a structured learning schedule ensures that skill enhancement becomes an integral part of your routine.

7. Exercise Regularly

Skill enhancement goes beyond theoretical knowledge—it requires practical application. Regular practice reinforces new skills and helps integrate them into your existing repertoire. Whether it's coding, public speaking, or project management, regular practice hones your abilities and ensures that you can apply them effectively in real-world scenarios.

8. Join Professional Associations

Become an active member of professional associations related to your industry. These associations often provide access to resources, networking opportunities, and events that can contribute to your continuous learning journey. Engaging with like-minded professionals fosters a collaborative environment for skill enhancement.

9. Embrace Cross-Disciplinary Learning

Explore knowledge beyond your immediate field of expertise. Cross-disciplinary learning introduces you to diverse perspectives and widens your skill set. The ability to draw connections between different disciplines enhances creativity and problem-solving abilities, making you a more versatile player in the game of success.

10. Reflect and Iterate

Regularly reflect on your learning journey. Identify what strategies and methods work best for you, celebrate achievements, and acknowledge areas for improvement. This reflective practice allows you to iterate on your approach, refining your learning strategies for continuous effectiveness.

Chapter 6: The Art of Resilience: Navigating the Game of Success

In the grand game of success, resilience is a game-changing attribute that can turn setbacks into stepping stones and challenges into opportunities. This chapter will explore the pivotal role of resilience, and how this dynamic skill can help individuals navigate the twists and turns of life.

Understanding Resilience as an Active Force

Resilience is not a passive quality; it's an active force that gives people the strength to overcome adversity, bounce back from difficulties, and adapt to changing circumstances. To succeed in the game of success, it's essential to understand resilience as an evolving skill. This involves cultivating the ability to endure, learn, and thrive in the face of challenges.

Navigating Setbacks with the Power of Resilience

Setbacks are unavoidable in the game of success, but it's how we respond to them that determines the course of our journey. Resilience can be a transformative power, allowing us to approach setbacks with a positive and forward-looking attitude. Instead of seeing them as defeats, resilient players view them as opportunities for growth and learning.

Anecdote: The Phoenix's Flight

Take the example of a business professional facing unexpected challenges in their career. Instead of giving in to despair, they embraced resilience as their guiding principle. Each setback became a chapter in their story of transformation. Through resilience, they not only overcame the challenges but emerged stronger, much like a phoenix rising from the ashes.

Developing a Resilient Mindset

Creating a resilient mindset involves believing in our ability to overcome obstacles. It's about reframing setbacks as temporary and viewing them as part of the game rather than insurmountable obstacles. A resilient mindset enables us to approach challenges with a solution-oriented perspective, focusing on what can be learned and gained from each experience.

Learning from Adversity: Resilience as a Teacher

Adversity can be a powerful teacher, and resilience is the student's willingness to learn. Resilient players recognize that every challenge presents an opportunity for growth. Whether facing professional setbacks, personal struggles, or unforeseen circumstances, the ability to extract lessons from adversity ensures that each experience contributes to personal and professional development.

Building Resilience Through Self-Care

Resilience is not just about enduring challenges but also about maintaining well-being. Incorporating self-care practices, such as mindfulness, adequate rest, and stress management, can help us stay strong in the face of challenges. A resilient player understands that taking care of oneself is not a luxury but a strategic move to ensure long-term success in the game.

Leveraging Support Systems

Resilience is often a collective effort. Building and leveraging support systems, such as personal relationships, mentorship, or professional networks, can help reinforce an individual's resilience. Knowing that you are not alone in the game and having a strong support system can enhance your ability to weather storms and emerge stronger on the other side.

The Iterative Cycle of Resilience

Resilience is not a one-time achievement but an iterative cycle. Each challenge faced and overcome contributes to the player's resilience, creating a continuous loop of growth and adaptation. The iterative nature of resilience ensures that players become increasingly adept at navigating the complex levels of the game.

These three individuals, Oprah Winfrey, Stephen Hawking, and Malala Yousafzai, have all demonstrated the remarkable strength of the human spirit. Despite facing adversity, each of them was able to overcome their struggles and reach new heights. Oprah, for example, was born into poverty and faced abuse and instability, yet she was able to transition from a local news anchor to a media mogul and philanthropist.

 Stephen Hawking was diagnosed with a debilitating neurological disease, yet he was able to continue his groundbreaking work in theoretical physics and write a best-selling book.

Malala was shot in the head for advocating girls' education, yet she recovered and went on to become the youngest-ever Nobel Prize laureate. These stories of resilience and courage are a testament to the power of the human spirit and serve as an inspiration to us all.

Building Resilience: Strategies for Triumph in the Game of Success

Resilience is not something you are born with; it is a skill that can be developed and strengthened over time. In this chapter, we will look at practical ways to build resilience, giving players the tools they need to face challenges, recover from setbacks, and come out stronger in the pursuit of success.

1. Cultivate a Positive Attitude

A positive attitude is the basis of resilience. Train your mind to focus on solutions rather than problems. See challenges as opportunities for growth and view setbacks as temporary obstacles rather than insurmountable ones. A positive outlook will help you approach adversity with a constructive and forward-looking attitude.

2. Create a Support Network

Building resilience is often a team effort. Surround yourself with a strong support system of friends, family, mentors, and peers who can provide guidance, encouragement, and a listening ear during difficult times. The strength of your support system can have a big impact on your ability to bounce back from adversity.

3. Embrace Change and Adaptability

Resilience involves being willing to adapt to change. Life is unpredictable, and the ability to adjust your strategies and perspectives in response to changing circumstances is essential. Embracing change allows you to navigate the unpredictable terrain of the game with flexibility and resilience.

4. Set Realistic Goals

Establishing realistic and achievable goals contributes to resilience. Break larger objectives into smaller, manageable tasks. This approach not only makes your goals more attainable but also gives you a roadmap for progress. Celebrate small victories along the way, reinforcing a sense of accomplishment and resilience.

5. Practice Self-Care

Taking care of your physical and mental health is an important part of resilience. Make time for self-care activities such as getting enough sleep, exercising regularly, and taking moments to relax. A resilient player knows that taking care of themselves is not a luxury but an investment in sustained success.

6. Develop Problem-Solving Skills

Resilience is closely linked to effective problem-solving. Improve your problem-solving skills by approaching challenges systematically. Break down complex issues into smaller components, identify possible solutions, and implement action plans. A proactive problem-solving approach will give you the confidence to navigate adversity.

7. Learn from Adversity

Every challenge presents an opportunity for learning and growth. Instead of viewing setbacks as failures, see them as valuable lessons. Reflect on the experiences, identify what you've learned, and consider how you can apply these insights to future situations. The ability to learn from adversity is a sign of a resilient player.

8. Foster Emotional Intelligence

Emotional intelligence, which includes self-awareness, empathy, and effective communication, enhances resilience. Understand and manage your emotions, navigate interpersonal dynamics, and build meaningful connections. Emotional intelligence gives you the tools to handle stress, communicate effectively, and recover from setbacks.

9. Maintain a Sense of Purpose

A sense of purpose provides a guiding light during difficult times. Clearly define your values, passions, and long-term objectives. Knowing your purpose gives you a sense of direction and meaning, helping you stay focused and resilient in the face of adversity.

10. Seek Professional Help

When faced with significant challenges, seeking professional help can be a valuable strategy for building resilience. Whether through counseling, coaching, or mentorship, professionals can offer specialized insights and support to navigate complex emotional and professional challenges.

Chapter 7: Game Over vs. New Levels: Embracing Continuity in the Game of Success

In the complex game of success, the idea of "game over" often arises, but the savvy player knows that it is not the end. Instead, it is a transition to new levels and fresh possibilities. This chapter looks at the idea that even when faced with difficulties or obstacles that feel like a "game over," there is always the potential for new levels, ongoing improvement, and the setting of inspiring new goals.

The concept of "game over" can be misleading. It may seem like a final point, where the journey ends and ambitions cease. However, in the ever-changing game of success, "game over" is more accurately a checkpoint—a moment to reflect, reevaluate, and adjust strategies. It is not the end, but a pause before the start of a new stage.

Those who are successful in the game of life have a continuous improvement mindset. Instead of viewing setbacks or perceived failures as definite conclusions, they see them as chances for refinement and growth. Every experience, whether positive or difficult, contributes to the iterative process of self-improvement.

Take the example of Thomas Edison, one of history's greatest inventors. In his quest to create the electric light bulb, Edison encountered many obstacles. Each time he faced an obstacle, he did not see it as a failure but as a discovery of how not to approach the problem. Edison's continuous improvement mindset eventually led to the invention of the long-lasting, practical electric light bulb.

In the game of success, setting new goals is like advancing to the next level. Goals give direction, purpose, and motivation. When faced with challenges that may seem like a temporary "game over," the act of envisioning and setting new goals becomes a transformative force. It pushes players forward, encouraging them to explore unknown territories and unlock new accomplishments.

Navigating new levels requires adaptability and resilience. The ability to learn from past experiences, adjust strategies, and accept change puts players in a position to thrive in unfamiliar terrain. Resilience becomes the armor that protects against the inevitable uncertainties, giving the courage to venture into unexplored levels with assurance.

Every new level brings a learning curve—a period of adjustment and exploration. Rather than being afraid of the difficulties of unfamiliar terrain, successful players embrace the learning curve. They understand that it is within the stretch of the curve that growth happens, and each phase of the journey adds to their developing skill set and wisdom.

Realizing the cyclical nature of success is essential to navigating the game effectively. The journey consists of highs and lows, successes and challenges. Knowing that "game over" moments are not permanent but part of a larger cycle allows players to approach setbacks with resilience and keep a steadfast commitment to continuous improvement.

Story 1: J.K. Rowling - From Difficulty to
Literary Acclaim

J.K. Rowling's rise to fame as the author of the
beloved Harry Potter series was not without its
struggles. After a difficult divorce and becoming
a single mother, Rowling faced poverty and
depression. Despite these hardships, she found
solace in writing and created the magical world
of Harry Potter.

Rowling's manuscript was rejected multiple
times before it was accepted. Her journey from a
struggling single mother to a celebrated author is
a testament to the power of resilience and
creativity. Through her determination and
imagination, she overcame her personal
struggles and created a cultural phenomenon that
continues to inspire millions.

Story 2: Jeff Bezos - Transforming Bookselling
into E-Commerce Supremacy

Jeff Bezos, the founder of Amazon, achieved one of the most remarkable business transformations of recent times. In the early 1990s, Bezos saw the potential of the internet and identified bookselling as a promising industry for online disruption. He left his successful job on Wall Street to pursue this vision, founding Amazon in his garage.

Amazon began as an online bookstore but quickly expanded its offerings, becoming an e-commerce giant that revolutionized the retail landscape. Bezos's bold reinvention and commitment to innovation transformed Amazon into a global technology and retail leader, demonstrating the transformative potential of embracing change.

Story 3: Steve Jobs - A Path of Innovation and Resilience

Steve Jobs, co-founder of Apple Inc., experienced a tumultuous journey of both successes and failures. After being removed from Apple in the mid-1980s, Jobs endured a period of professional exile. Despite this, he founded NeXT and Pixar, both of which eventually became successful ventures.

Jobs's return to Apple marked a historic turnaround. With products like the iMac, iPod, iPhone, and iPad, he redefined industries and solidified Apple's status as an innovation leader. Jobs's story shows how setbacks and reinvention can lead to extraordinary accomplishments, highlighting the transformative power of resilience and unwavering vision.

Story 4: Michelle Obama - Redefining Roles and Influence

Michelle Obama, former First Lady of the United States, embarked on a journey of reinvention and purpose. Initially a lawyer, Michelle transitioned into public service and advocacy. As First Lady, she focused on issues such as education, health, and military families, using her platform to promote social causes.

Post-White House, Michelle continued her commitment to education and empowerment. She wrote a bestselling memoir, "Becoming," and launched initiatives like the "Let's Move!" campaign. Michelle's story demonstrates how individuals can redefine their roles, leveraging their influence for positive change and leaving a lasting impact on society.

Chapter 8: Multiplayer Mode - Collaboration and Networking: The Synergy of Success

In the intricate and complex game of success, the concept of "Multiplayer Mode" is a powerful strategy—collaboration and networking. This chapter explores the importance of connecting with others, forming alliances, and engaging in collective endeavors. In the multiplayer mode of success, synergy is the key to achieving both individual and collective triumphs.

The power of collective intelligence is greater than individual capabilities. Working with a variety of minds brings a wealth of perspectives, ideas, and expertise to the table. The synergy created by combining knowledge and skills boosts the game, leading to creative solutions and improved problem-solving.

Success is rarely achieved alone. Forming a supportive alliance through collaboration and networking provides a strong foundation. Allies offer encouragement, share insights, and provide a safety net during difficult times. A well-forged alliance is a valuable asset, amplifying individual strengths and fostering a sense of camaraderie in the game.

Networking is not just a social activity—it's a strategic move in the game of success. Establishing and nurturing professional connections opens doors to opportunities, insights, and collaborations. Networking creates a web of relationships that can influence career trajectories, introduce new possibilities, and enhance the player's overall gameplay.

Take the example of a group of tech entrepreneurs who, through strategic networking, formed a roundtable to share industry insights and collaborate on ventures. This collaborative effort not only accelerated individual business growth but also led to the development of groundbreaking technologies through the synergy of their collective expertise.

In multiplayer mode, each player brings unique strengths to the game. Collaborative endeavors allow individuals to leverage their respective strengths, creating a dynamic synergy that propels the team forward. Recognizing and valuing the strengths of each player fosters an environment of mutual support and collective achievement.

Networking and collaboration facilitate the cross-pollination of ideas—an exchange that sparks creativity and innovation. Exposure to diverse perspectives, industries, and approaches broadens players' horizons, inspiring fresh thinking and novel solutions. The cross-pollination of ideas is a catalyst for staying ahead in the ever-evolving game of success.

In the multiplayer mode, mentorship plays a pivotal role. Experienced players, acting as mentors, offer guidance, share experiences, and provide insights that accelerate the learning curve for those navigating the game. Mentorship fosters a culture of continuous learning and growth, ensuring that players are well-equipped to tackle new challenges.

Challenges in the game of success are often multifaceted, requiring collaborative problem-solving. A team of players, each contributing their expertise, can dissect complex issues and devise comprehensive solutions. Collaborative problem-solving not only enhances efficiency but also reinforces the resilience of the collective.

** The Benefits of Building Meaningful
Connections: Networking for Success**

In the game of success, building meaningful
connections is essential for achieving success.
This chapter explores the advantages of
networking and collaboration, providing tips on
how to effectively forge and nurture
connections. Doing so will help players not only
survive but thrive in the ever-changing
landscape of the game.

The benefits of building meaningful connections
are numerous. Firstly, it provides access to a
variety of opportunities, from career
advancements to collaborative ventures.
Secondly, it facilitates the exchange of
knowledge and insights, allowing players to
broaden their perspectives and learn from others.
Thirdly, it provides emotional support, allowing
players to rely on a network of individuals who
understand and empathize with them. Fourthly, it
can lead to career advancement, providing
opportunities for mentorship, professional

development, and career growth. Fifthly, it enables collaboration and synergy, allowing players to leverage collective strengths and propel each other to new levels of success. Sixthly, it brings together individuals with diverse perspectives and experiences, enriching decision-making processes and fueling creativity. Lastly, it increases visibility in professional circles, leading to invitations, partnerships, and opportunities that contribute to overall success.

To effectively network and collaborate, players should be genuine and authentic in their interactions, attend networking events, utilize online platforms, offer value first, cultivate active listening, seek mentorship, attend networking groups, follow up and stay connected, be open to collaboration, and build a diverse network. Doing so will help players reap the rewards of building meaningful connections and achieve success in the game of success.

Chapter 9: Power-Ups and Boosts - Taking Advantage of Opportunities

In the complex game of success, opportunities can be seen as powerful catalysts, similar to power-ups and boosts that can help players reach new heights. This chapter looks into the idea of opportunities as game-changers, exploring how players can identify, take advantage of, and make the most of these power-ups to progress in the dynamic and rewarding world of the game.

Recognizing Opportunities as Power-Ups:

In the game of success, opportunities can be seen as power-ups—special advantages that, when taken advantage of, can improve a player's position and trajectory. Just like a well-timed power-up can change the course of a video game, strategically recognizing and utilizing opportunities can take a player's journey to unprecedented levels of success.

The Dynamic Nature of Opportunities:

Opportunities are ever-changing and always present, similar to power-ups that appear strategically throughout a game. Understanding the fleeting nature of opportunities emphasizes the importance of being attentive and prepared, making sure that players are ready to take advantage of these moments that can have a major impact on their gameplay.

Seizing the Right Moment:

To make the most of opportunities, players need to have a good sense of timing. Players must be aware of the nuances of the game, recognizing when a particular power-up is within reach. This involves a combination of strategic foresight, situational awareness, and the ability to act quickly when the moment presents itself.

Strategic Decision-Making:

Opportunities often require strategic decision-making. Players must consider the potential risks and rewards, evaluating the effect of each decision on their overall gameplay. Just like selecting the right power-up can enhance a character's abilities, making informed choices when opportunities arise can increase a player's chances of success.

Maximizing the Impact:

To really benefit from power-ups, players must maximize their impact. Similarly, taking advantage of opportunities is not enough; players must actively use them to move their journey forward. This may involve collaboration, innovation, or a strategic shift in approach—making sure that the full potential of the opportunity is realized.

Anecdote: The Entrepreneur's Windfall

Think of the story of an entrepreneur who, during a period of economic downturn, noticed an opportunity to buy out struggling competitors. By strategically taking advantage of this power-up, the entrepreneur not only increased their market share but also put their business in a position for unprecedented growth during the subsequent economic upturn.

Learning from Setbacks:

Not all opportunities will lead to immediate success. Some might result in setbacks or unexpected challenges. However, viewing setbacks as valuable lessons can help a player become more resilient and adaptable. Learning from the outcomes of seized opportunities ensures continuous improvement in the game.

The Cumulative Effect of Opportunities:

In the game of success, each successfully taken advantage of opportunity contributes to a player's overall progress. Just like accumulating power-ups can enhance a character's abilities, capitalizing on a series of opportunities can help players move through successive levels of achievement, creating a cumulative effect that shapes their journey.

Recognizing and Seizing Opportunities: The Art of Strategic Gameplay

In the ever-changing game of success, the ability to recognize and take advantage of opportunities is a skill that sets the most successful players apart. This chapter looks at the art of strategic gameplay, offering insights on how to identify opportunities and capitalize on them effectively. Through stories of individuals who made the most of unexpected opportunities, we can see the transformative power of seizing the right moments in the intricate game of life.

Developing Opportunistic Awareness is key to recognizing opportunities. Successful players are attuned to changes in their environment, industry trends, and emerging possibilities. This involves staying informed, seeking diverse perspectives, and having a mindset of continuous curiosity.

Adapting to change is also important, as opportunities often arise in the midst of it. Players who are open to embracing new circumstances are better placed to recognize and take advantage of these openings. This requires a willingness to step outside comfort zones, explore uncharted territories, and view uncertainties not as obstacles but as potential sources of opportunity.

Networking and collaboration are powerful tools for opportunity recognition. Players who actively engage with diverse networks often gain early insights into emerging trends and potential collaborations. The collective intelligence within a network can help identify opportunities that might be invisible to those operating in isolation.

The story of two entrepreneurs attending the same networking event is a great example of how chance encounters can lead to strategic partnerships, unlocking unforeseen opportunities and propelling both entrepreneurs to new levels of success.

Some of the most impactful opportunities are unplanned and unexpected. Players who remain open to the unplanned events, chance encounters, and unforeseen circumstances are better positioned to seize these opportunities. This involves maintaining flexibility and the ability to pivot when unexpected possibilities arise.

Seizing opportunities often involves an element of strategic risk-taking. Calculated risks, informed by thorough analysis and a clear understanding of potential outcomes, can lead to significant rewards. Successful players assess the risks associated with each opportunity and make informed decisions based on their strategic goals.

Setbacks may occur, but resilient players view these setbacks as valuable lessons. Learning from the outcomes of seized opportunities contributes to continuous improvement, refining players' ability to assess, strategize, and capitalize on future openings.

Unexpected circumstances can be the breeding ground for unique opportunities. Players who can leverage these unexpected turns of events by remaining adaptable and creative find themselves at an advantage. The ability to turn challenges into opportunities is a hallmark of strategic gameplay in the game of success.

Stories of Opportunity Seizure include Instagram's pivot from a location-sharing app to a photo-sharing platform, Howard Schultz's recognition of the opportunity to create a coffeehouse experience in the US, and Twitter's unexpected birth from a failed podcast platform.

Story 1: Slack - From Gaming to Workplace
Communication

Stewart Butterfield and his team had an
unexpected journey to success. Initially, they
were developing an online game called "Glitch,"
but when it faced challenges, they decided to
create an internal communication platform
instead. Little did they know that this platform,
which later became Slack, would revolutionize
workplace communication. This unexpected
shift from gaming to collaboration transformed a
setback into a groundbreaking opportunity,
making Slack one of the most widely used
communication tools in the business world.

Story 2: FedEx - A Last-Minute Lifeline

Fred Smith, the founder of FedEx, was in a
critical situation when the company was on the
brink of bankruptcy. With only $5,000 left in
funds, Smith traveled to Las Vegas and gambled,
hoping to win enough money to cover the

company's fuel bill. Miraculously, he succeeded, winning $27,000 and saving FedEx. This unexpected and high-stakes opportunity not only saved the company but also laid the foundation for its future success as a global shipping giant.

Story 3: YouTube - A Video Dating Site Turns Video-Sharing Platform

YouTube, now a cornerstone of online video content, began as a dating site called "Tune In Hook Up." The platform allowed users to upload videos describing their ideal partners. However, when the dating aspect failed to gain traction, the founders noticed users were sharing a different kind of content—videos of various interests and experiences. Realizing this unexpected usage, YouTube pivoted to become a video-sharing platform. This shift transformed YouTube into a cultural phenomenon, providing a platform for content creators and changing the way we consume video content.

Story 4: Post-it Notes - A Failed Adhesive
Becomes a Sticky Success

Spencer Silver, a chemist at 3M, stumbled upon
a unique adhesive that, instead of bonding
strongly, only created a weak temporary bond.
Initially seen as a failed product, Arthur Fry,
another 3M employee, realized the potential of
this weak adhesive for creating bookmarks in his
hymnal. Together, they turned this unexpected
discovery into what we now know as Post-it
Notes. The accidental invention became a global
success and an essential tool for note-taking and
organization.

Story 5: WD-40 - Water Displacement Becomes
a Multi-Use Product

WD-40, a popular lubricant and rust preventive,
originated from an attempt to create a formula to
displace water. The 40th attempt led to the
creation of WD-40, but its initial purpose as a
water displacer was not as successful as
expected. However, employees noticed its

effectiveness for various applications, from loosening rusty bolts to preventing corrosion. This unexpected versatility turned WD-40 into a household name and a staple in many toolboxes.

Chapter 10: The Hidden Levels - Exploring Uncharted Territories

In the complex and ever-changing game of success, there are hidden levels that await those who are willing to take the plunge and explore beyond the familiar. This chapter invites players to take on the exciting challenge of venturing into uncharted territories—those unexplored realms where the extraordinary often lies in wait. Stepping out of one's comfort zone is the key to unlocking hidden levels and uncovering untold possibilities in the grand and dynamic game of life.

The Comfort Zone Conundrum:

Comfort zones can be comforting, but they can also be restrictive. Like a confined area in a game, they can prevent players from accessing the full range of experiences and opportunities.

Acknowledging the comfort zone conundrum is the first step to taking on the adventure of exploring uncharted territories.

Embracing Discomfort as Growth:

Hidden levels often come with discomfort and uncertainty. However, it is within this discomfort that players find the elements necessary for growth and progress. Encouraging readers to view discomfort as a sign of potential growth changes the narrative, transforming challenges into stepping stones towards new accomplishments.

The Thrill of the Unknown:

Exploring uncharted territories adds an element of excitement to the game. The unknown becomes a platform for innovation, creativity, and self-discovery. Players who embrace the thrill of uncertainty discover hidden levels where the rules are rewritten, and new possibilities emerge.

Learning Through Exploration:

Just as characters in a game acquire new skills
and knowledge by exploring different levels,
individuals in the game of success learn through
exploration. Stepping into uncharted territories
expands perspectives, introduces fresh insights,
and cultivates a mindset of continuous
learning—an invaluable asset on the journey to
success.

Overcoming Fear and Resistance:

Fear and resistance often come with the prospect
of stepping into the unknown. Acknowledging
these emotions and understanding that they are
natural reactions gives players the power to
confront and overcome them. The hidden levels
of success are often guarded by fear, and it takes
courage to uncover their secrets.

Pioneering Innovation:

Hidden levels are ideal for innovation. Pioneers who dare to explore uncharted territories in their industries, careers, or personal lives often uncover innovative solutions and approaches. Encouraging readers to become pioneers in their respective domains ignites a spirit of creativity and ingenuity.

Cultivating Resilience:

Hidden levels may present unexpected challenges, requiring resilience to navigate successfully. Every obstacle encountered in uncharted territories becomes an opportunity for players to develop and strengthen their resilience—a crucial attribute for sustained success in the ever-evolving game.

Redefining Success:

Exploring uncharted territories allows players to redefine their ideas of success. Rather than adhering to conventional standards, individuals who embark on this journey discover that

success can take many forms. It becomes a
personalized quest, shaped by the unique
experiences and achievements encountered in
the hidden levels.

Inviting Serendipity:

Serendipity often accompanies exploration.
Unexpected encounters, chance discoveries, and
unanticipated opportunities may present
themselves when players venture beyond their
comfort zones. Embracing the concept of
inviting serendipity encourages readers to stay
open to the unexpected treasures hidden in
uncharted territories.

** The Rewards of Exploration - Unveiling the Benefits of New Territories and Risks

In the grand game of success, the rewards of venturing into new territories and taking risks are limitless. This chapter sheds light on the incredible benefits that await those who dare to step out of their comfort zone and embrace the unknown. From personal growth to unprecedented accomplishments, the journey into uncharted realms can be a life-changing experience.

Personal growth and development are just some of the advantages of exploring new territories. Beyond the familiar lies the potential to discover untapped abilities, acquire new skills, and cultivate a mindset of continuous learning. The challenges encountered in unfamiliar places can help build resilience and adaptability, making players more capable and formidable.

New territories also provide a breeding ground for innovation and creativity. The novel obstacles and unfamiliar landscapes can spark the imagination, inspiring players to think outside the box. It is in these unexplored realms that groundbreaking ideas, solutions, and approaches often emerge, leading to advancements in various fields.

Venturing into new territories also broadens perspectives and deepens understanding of the world. Exposure to different cultures, ideas, and experiences can enhance players' insights, fostering a more inclusive and comprehensive worldview. This expanded perspective can be a valuable asset in navigating the complexities of the game.

The learning curve in uncharted territories is often steep, resulting in accelerated personal and professional development. Players can acquire skills and knowledge at a faster rate, giving them a competitive edge in their respective domains. The challenges encountered can also be valuable lessons that contribute to an enriched skill set and a more profound understanding of their chosen paths.

New territories can also conceal opportunities for breakthroughs and unprecedented achievements. Players who take calculated risks can seize these hidden opportunities, propelling them to new heights of success. The willingness to venture into the unknown can be a strategic move that can lead to game-changing triumphs.

Successfully navigating uncharted territories and overcoming challenges can also boost self-confidence. Players can discover their capacity to tackle the unknown, leading to a heightened belief in their abilities. This newfound confidence can be a driving force, empowering them to take on even greater challenges in the game.

Exploring new territories also allows players to create a unique legacy. By venturing beyond established norms and taking risks, individuals can leave their mark on the game of success. The stories of those who dared to explore uncharted realms can become inspirational tales, influencing and inspiring future players in the grand and ever-evolving game of life.

Story 1: Elon Musk - Transforming Multiple Industries

Elon Musk, a visionary entrepreneur, is renowned for his willingness to take risks and transform multiple industries. Musk co-founded PayPal, an early leader in online payments, before taking on the challenge of space exploration with SpaceX. Despite initial doubts and setbacks, SpaceX succeeded in developing reusable rockets, significantly reducing the cost of space travel. Musk then set his sights on electric vehicles, founding Tesla, a company that revolutionized the automotive industry by popularizing electric cars. Musk's ambitious ventures demonstrate how taking risks and embracing the unknown can lead to remarkable success across a variety of sectors.

Story 2: Oprah Winfrey - From Local News to Global Impact

Oprah Winfrey, a media mogul, embraced the unknown and took risks that led to her meteoric rise. Early in her career, Oprah transitioned from local news reporting to co-hosting a local talk show, People Are Talking. However, her real breakthrough came when she took on the challenge of hosting a struggling Chicago morning talk show, which she transformed into The Oprah Winfrey Show. The show's success catapulted Oprah to international fame, making her one of the most influential and successful media personalities of all time. Oprah's fearlessness in pursuing the unknown and her willingness to take risks reshaped the landscape of talk shows and media, leaving an indelible mark on the industry.

Story 3: James Cameron - Exploring the Abyss and Beyond

James Cameron, a renowned filmmaker and explorer, is celebrated for his contributions to cinema and deep-sea exploration. Cameron's fascination with the unknown led him to create groundbreaking films like Titanic and Avatar, both of which set records and redefined cinematic possibilities. Beyond filmmaking, Cameron embraced the literal unknown by venturing into the depths of the ocean. In 2012, he piloted the Deepsea Challenger to the Mariana Trench's Challenger Deep, the deepest known point in Earth's oceans. Cameron's journey into the abyss illustrates how embracing the unknown, both creatively and literally, can lead to unparalleled success and groundbreaking achievements.

Story 4: Malala Yousafzai - A Voice for Education in the Face of Adversity

Malala Yousafzai, a Pakistani education activist, became a global symbol of courage by embracing the unknown and standing up for girls' education in the face of adversity. Malala survived a Taliban assassination attempt for her advocacy and continued to speak out, eventually becoming the youngest-ever recipient of the Nobel Peace Prize. Her willingness to confront the unknown and speak out against injustice turned her into an international symbol of resilience and an advocate for educational opportunities for girls worldwide.

Story 5: Richard Branson - From Music to Space Travel

Sir Richard Branson, a British entrepreneur, exemplifies success through embracing the unknown and taking bold risks. Branson began with a mail-order record business before founding Virgin Records, which signed iconic artists like the Rolling Stones and Janet Jackson. Undeterred by skepticism, Branson expanded into numerous industries, including airlines, trains, and telecommunications, creating the Virgin Group. In recent years, he ventured into the unknown once again with Virgin Galactic, aiming to make commercial space travel a reality. Branson's varied journey showcases how taking risks and embracing uncertainty can lead to multifaceted success.

Chapter 11: Boss Battles - Facing Major Challenges

In the complex game of success, there are certain obstacles that can be likened to "boss battles"—formidable challenges that require strategic thinking, resilience, and a heightened level of skill to overcome. This chapter will explore the major challenges that can be compared to boss battles, looking at their impact on players and offering advice on how to navigate these difficult encounters in the dynamic and rewarding game of life.

Financial issues often present themselves as boss battles, testing a person's resourcefulness and financial knowledge. From unexpected costs to economic downturns, managing financial setbacks requires careful budgeting, flexibility, and the ability to make wise financial decisions under pressure.

Changing careers or facing unexpected shifts in professional paths can be likened to a boss battle. Players must adjust their skill sets, explore unfamiliar industries, and strategically position themselves to succeed in new professional environments.

The deep impact of personal loss and grief can be seen as a boss battle in the game of life. Navigating the emotional complexities, finding strength, and maintaining a sense of purpose in the face of great loss requires tremendous strength and emotional intelligence.

Health issues, whether personal or for loved ones, can be a formidable boss battle. Players must understand the complexities of healthcare, make important decisions about treatment, and cultivate mental and emotional resilience to cope with the physical and emotional toll of health-related struggles.

Starting and sustaining entrepreneurial ventures can be compared to boss battles in the business world. Entrepreneurs must deal with uncertainties, market dynamics, and intense competition. Succeeding in entrepreneurship requires strategic thinking, adaptability, and the ability to persist through difficulties.

Dealing with significant relationship issues can be seen as boss battles in the personal domain. Whether it's conflicts with family members, friends, or romantic partners, players must use effective communication, empathy, and conflict resolution skills to overcome relationship challenges.

Mental health issues, such as anxiety, depression, or other mental health conditions, are formidable boss battles that require players to prioritize self-care, seek professional help, and develop coping mechanisms to manage the intricacies of mental health struggles.

Players may also encounter boss battles on a global scale, such as navigating economic recessions, political instability, or environmental crises. Successfully facing these challenges requires a global perspective, strategic thinking, and collaborative efforts to bring about positive change.

Major life transitions, such as retirement, becoming a parent, or adapting to an empty nest, can be seen as boss battles that require players to adjust to new roles, redefine priorities, and find purpose in changing life stages.

Finding a harmonious balance between work and personal life is an ongoing boss battle. Players must manage the demands of professional responsibilities while nurturing relationships, maintaining health and well-being, and finding fulfillment outside of the workplace.

Take, for example, the story of someone facing substantial financial setbacks due to unforeseen circumstances. This player strategically overcame the challenge by creating a comprehensive financial plan, exploring new revenue streams, and leveraging their skills to regain financial stability. The financial resurgence was a testament to their strategic prowess in overcoming a boss battle.

Triumph Strategies - Overcoming Significant Obstacles

In the complex game of life, players often face significant obstacles—boss battles that test their mettle and determination. This chapter explores strategies for success, offering insights and approaches to help players overcome formidable challenges and come out victorious.

Strategic planning is key. Break down the obstacle into manageable tasks, create a plan of action, and set realistic goals. This provides a roadmap for navigating complexities and instills a sense of control. Resilience and adaptability are also essential. Embrace the understanding that setbacks are part of the game, and the ability to bounce back and adjust to changing circumstances is invaluable.

Don't go it alone. Seek support from friends, family, mentors, or professional networks. Collaborative efforts can provide diverse perspectives, shared insights, and emotional support. Leverage the strength of a supportive community to navigate obstacles more effectively.

Continuous learning and skill development are also important. Use obstacles as opportunities to acquire new skills and knowledge. The process of overcoming challenges often necessitates personal and professional growth. View each obstacle as a chance to enhance your skill set, making you more adept at facing future challenges.

Maintain a positive mindset and visualize success. The power of positive thinking can influence your approach to challenges. Visualization techniques, where you vividly imagine overcoming obstacles and achieving success, can foster a proactive and optimistic mindset.

When faced with a complex challenge, break it down into smaller, more manageable components. Addressing individual aspects sequentially allows for a more focused and systematic approach. Tackling smaller tasks incrementally builds momentum toward overcoming the larger obstacle.

Be flexible in your approach to challenges. If a particular strategy proves ineffective, be willing to adapt and explore alternative solutions. Flexibility allows players to navigate unforeseen obstacles and adjust their strategies in real-time.

Time management is also essential. Prioritize tasks based on urgency and importance. Time management ensures that efforts are directed toward the most critical aspects of overcoming an obstacle, preventing the feeling of being overwhelmed by the sheer magnitude of the challenge.

Innovate and think outside the box. Consider unconventional solutions and approaches to overcome obstacles. Breakthrough innovation often arises when players challenge traditional methods and explore new ways of addressing challenges.

After overcoming an obstacle or facing a setback, take the time to reflect and learn. Analyze what worked well, what could be improved, and how you can apply these insights to future challenges. Continuous reflection contributes to ongoing personal and professional development.

Take the example of an entrepreneur faced with a market shift that rendered their initial business model less viable. Instead of succumbing to the challenge, they embraced the opportunity for innovation. Through strategic planning, collaboration with industry experts, and a positive mindset, they successfully pivoted their business model, ultimately thriving in the face of adversity.

Inspiring Stories of Triumph Over Boss Battles:

1. **J.K. Rowling - From Rejection to Literary Success:**
   - Before becoming one of the most renowned authors in history, J.K. Rowling experienced numerous rejections for her first Harry Potter manuscript. Despite financial difficulties and personal struggles, Rowling persevered and her hard work paid off when the series became a worldwide sensation, transforming her into a literary icon and demonstrating the power of resilience and creativity.

2. **Steve Jobs - Redemption and Innovation:**
   - Steve Jobs, co-founder of Apple Inc., encountered a formidable challenge when he was removed from his own company in 1985. Undeterred, Jobs established NeXT and Pixar Animation Studios. In a remarkable turnaround, he returned to Apple in 1997, leading the company to unprecedented success with

revolutionary products such as the iPod, iPhone, and iPad. Jobs' story illustrates the victory of vision, innovation, and tenacity over obstacles.

3. **Malcolm X - Transformation and Advocacy:**
   - Malcolm X, a prominent figure in the American Civil Rights Movement, faced personal and societal difficulties throughout his life. From a troubled youth to imprisonment, Malcolm X underwent a transformative journey in prison, leading him to embrace Islam. He emerged as a powerful advocate for Black rights, challenging societal norms and contributing to the Civil Rights Movement. His story reflects the strength to overcome personal adversities and drive change on a larger scale.

4. **Rosa Parks - The Quiet Strength of Defiance:**
   - Rosa Parks, known as the "mother of the civil rights movement," encountered a major challenge on a bus in Montgomery, Alabama, in 1955. Her refusal to give up her seat to a white

passenger sparked the Montgomery Bus Boycott
and became a symbol of resistance against racial
segregation. Parks' quiet strength and
determination played a crucial role in the fight
for civil rights.

5. **Nick Vujicic - Turning Limitations into
Inspiration:**
   - Born without limbs, Nick Vujicic faced
extraordinary difficulties. Bullied and struggling
with depression, he contemplated suicide.
However, Nick turned his life around, embracing
his differences and becoming a motivational
speaker. Through his organization, Life Without
Limbs, Nick motivates millions around the
world, demonstrating that the human spirit can
overcome physical limitations.

6. **Bethany Hamilton - Surfing Against the
Odds:**
   - Professional surfer Bethany Hamilton faced a
life-altering challenge when she lost her left arm
in a shark attack at the age of 13. Unfazed by the
setback, Bethany returned to competitive

surfing, eventually winning championships. Her resilience and determination not only brought her personal triumph but also inspired many facing their own battles.

7. **Winston Churchill - Leadership in Times of Crisis:**
   - Winston Churchill, the Prime Minister of the United Kingdom during World War II, faced the daunting task of leading his nation through one of its darkest periods. His unyielding resolve, eloquent speeches, and strategic leadership played a pivotal role in guiding Britain to victory. Churchill's resilience and courage in the face of adversity remain an enduring example of leadership under pressure.

Chapter 12: Redefining Success - Beyond Conventional Measures

In the complex game of life, many people find themselves confined to traditional definitions of success. This chapter encourages individuals to redefine success on their own terms.

 By exploring different metrics and perspectives, they can create a personal scoreboard that reflects their unique journey, values, and goals in the dynamic and rewarding game of life. Questioning conventional metrics is the first step. Instead of relying on external validation, ask yourself if traditional markers such as wealth, status, or societal approval truly align with your personal values and fulfillment.

Redefining success means aligning your pursuits with your core values. What brings you joy, fulfillment, and a sense of purpose? Success,

when measured against personal values,
becomes a more authentic and meaningful
pursuit. It's also important to consider the
holistic aspects of your life, including
relationships, well-being, personal growth, and
community contributions.

 Balancing these dimensions contributes to a
more comprehensive and satisfying definition of
success. Success is a journey, not a destination.
Embrace the concept of individual progress,
recognizing that each step forward, no matter
how small, contributes to your overall success.
This perspective encourages a focus on
continuous improvement and personal growth.
Intrinsic motivation is also key.

Find joy and satisfaction in the process of
pursuing your goals, rather than relying solely
on external rewards or recognition. Well-being is
also a crucial component of success. Mental,
emotional, and physical health contribute
significantly to a fulfilling life. Redefine success
by placing well-being at the forefront.

Additionally, success isn't solely an individual pursuit—it thrives in meaningful connections with others. Valuing and nurturing relationships is an important part of redefining success. Finally, consider success in the context of contributing to a greater purpose. How does your journey positively impact the world around you? Redefine success by acknowledging the significance of your contributions to the community, society, or causes that align with your values.

Celebrate unconventional successes—moments of resilience, learning, and overcoming challenges. Redefining success involves acknowledging and valuing the less visible yet profoundly impactful aspects of your journey. Success is a deeply personal narrative. Craft your own story by embracing the uniqueness of your journey.

Redefine success by recognizing that your path, with all its twists and turns, contributes to a narrative that is exclusively yours.

** Your Score, Your Game - Defining Personal Metrics for Success**

In the ever-changing game of life, you have the power to design your own scoreboard. This chapter encourages you to break away from traditional standards and take control of creating your own definition of success. By embracing your individual values, goals, and journey, you can create a personalized scoreboard that reflects the game you want to play and the success you desire.

1. **Reflect on Your Values:

Start by reflecting on your core values. What principles guide your decisions, actions, and aspirations? Identifying and embracing your values is the first step in creating a scoreboard that is true to your authentic self.

2. **Clarify Your Aspirations:

Think about your aspirations, both short-term and long-term. What do you envision for yourself in various aspects of life—career, relationships, personal growth, and well-being? Clarifying your aspirations gives you a clear direction for defining success on your own terms.

3. **Challenge External Expectations:

Challenge external expectations and societal norms that may not align with your values and aspirations. Remember that success is a subjective concept and doesn't have a universal definition. By questioning external pressures, you can reclaim the autonomy to define your own metrics.

4. **Balance Multiple Dimensions:

View success as a multi-dimensional concept. Explore how achievements in different areas of your life contribute to your overall well-being and fulfillment. Balancing multiple dimensions allows you to create a more comprehensive and satisfying definition of success.

5. **Prioritize Well-Being:

Put well-being at the top of your scoreboard. Consider how your pursuits contribute to your mental, emotional, and physical health. Prioritizing well-being ensures that your journey toward success is sustainable and fulfilling.

6. **Celebrate Individual Progress:

Shift your focus from external benchmarks to individual progress. Acknowledge and celebrate each step forward, understanding that success is a continuous journey of growth and learning. By valuing progress, you can foster a positive and motivating mindset.

7. **Cultivate Intrinsic Motivation:

Look within for motivation. Cultivate intrinsic motivation by finding joy and satisfaction in the

process of pursuing your goals. This internal
drive becomes a resilient source of fulfillment,
allowing you to face challenges with purpose
and passion.

8. **Nurture Meaningful Connections:

Recognize the importance of relationships in
your success story. Cultivate and nurture
meaningful connections with others. The impact
you have on those around you, and the shared
experiences you create, are essential components
of your personal scoreboard.

9. **Contribute to a Greater Purpose:

Explore how your journey aligns with a greater
purpose. Think about the positive impact you
can have on the community, society, or causes
that resonate with your values. Redefine success
by recognizing the meaningful contributions you
make to the world around you.

10. **Craft Your Unique Narrative:

Your journey is a unique narrative. Craft your story by embracing the uniqueness of your path. Your triumphs, challenges, and the lessons learned contribute to a narrative that is exclusively yours—a narrative that defines success on your terms.

Reflect on Your Journey:

Think about moments in your life where you felt a profound sense of accomplishment, fulfillment, or joy. What were the circumstances, and what values were in play? These reflections can help you understand your own metrics for success.

The Heart of the Game - Prioritizing Personal Fulfillment and Happiness

In the grand game of life, personal fulfillment and happiness are the ultimate measures of success. This chapter emphasizes the importance of prioritizing these intrinsic elements, as true success is not just about achieving external goals, but about cultivating a sense of joy, purpose, and contentment within the dynamic and rewarding game of life.

The essence of personal fulfillment is that it goes beyond external accomplishments. It is the deep satisfaction that comes from aligning your actions, choices, and pursuits with your core values and aspirations. Fulfillment is achieved when your journey is in line with who you are and the impact you wish to make.

Happiness is a powerful force that drives motivation, resilience, and a positive attitude. When happiness is a central metric for success, the pursuit of goals is filled with joy, making the journey as meaningful as the destination.

Prioritizing personal fulfillment and happiness means maintaining balance in all aspects of life. This includes nurturing relationships, fostering well-being, and finding equilibrium between professional pursuits and personal joys. Balance is the foundation for sustained happiness.

Achieving personal fulfillment requires authenticity and self-discovery. Embrace your true self, explore your passions, and gain a deeper understanding of what brings you genuine joy. The journey of self-discovery is a vital part of the game, leading to a more authentic and fulfilling life.

Prioritizing personal fulfillment gives you the resilience to face challenges. When happiness is intertwined with your pursuits, setbacks become opportunities for growth rather than insurmountable obstacles. Resilience is a natural result of a fulfilling and joyous journey.

Personal fulfillment is often connected to meaningful connections. Cultivate relationships that bring joy, support, and a sense of belonging. Meaningful connections contribute immensely to your overall happiness and add to the richness of the game.

Discovering and living with purpose amplifies personal fulfillment. Understand the impact you wish to make on the world and align your actions with that purpose. Contributing to a greater good is a source of profound fulfillment and lasting happiness.

Integrate gratitude into your daily practice. Reflect on the positive aspects of your journey, acknowledging the achievements, experiences, and relationships that bring joy. Gratitude encourages a positive mindset and increases your capacity for personal fulfillment.

Embrace change as a catalyst for personal growth and fulfillment. Recognize that the game is dynamic, with changing goals and aspirations. Embracing change allows you to adapt, learn, and continually align your journey with what brings you lasting joy and fulfillment.

Amidst the pursuit of goals, savor the present moment. Happiness is not only linked to future achievements; it flourishes in the small, everyday joys. Embrace mindfulness and the art of being present, allowing yourself to fully experience and appreciate the richness of the game in the now.

Take a moment to think about times in your life when you felt truly joyous and fulfilled. What were you doing, who were you with, and what values were in play? These reflections can help you prioritize personal fulfillment and happiness in your ongoing journey.

Chapter 13: Game Analytics - Reflecting on Your Journey

In the complex game of life, progress isn't just about moving forward, but also about taking the time to reflect on the path you've taken. This chapter introduces the concept of game analytics, which encourages players to assess themselves and learn from their experiences. By recognizing the power of reflection, individuals can gain valuable insights, refine their strategies, and navigate the dynamic and rewarding game of life more intentionally.

Self-assessment is an art form. Take the time to evaluate your progress, successes, and struggles. Think about how your actions align with your goals. Self-assessment can be a compass that guides you through the intricate game.

Every experience, whether it's a success or a setback, has something to teach you. Embrace the importance of learning from your experiences. What went well? What could be improved? By taking away lessons from your journey, you can better prepare yourself for future challenges.

Game analytics involve recognizing patterns and trends in your behavior, decisions, and outcomes. Notice any recurring themes and consider their impact on your progress. Understanding patterns gives you the knowledge to make informed adjustments and optimize your strategies.

Don't forget to take a moment to celebrate your milestones. Acknowledge and appreciate your accomplishments, both big and small. Celebrating milestones not only boosts morale, but also gives you a sense of accomplishment, which can help keep you motivated.

Reflection can also prompt you to adjust your strategies. If certain approaches are working, think about how to make them even better. On the other hand, if you're facing challenges, explore alternative strategies. Adapting and refining your strategies based on reflection is a key part of successful gameplay.

Evaluate how your actions align with your core values. Are your pursuits in line with what's important to you? Reflecting on your values ensures that your journey remains true to yourself, which can lead to a more meaningful and purposeful game.

Reflection can also help you course-correct when needed. If you find yourself straying from your desired path, look at it as an opportunity to redirect yourself. Resilience comes from the ability to adjust and persist with newfound knowledge.

Incorporate mindfulness into your gameplay. Being present in each moment allows for more intentional reflection. Mindfulness can help you appreciate the nuances of your journey, which can lead to a deeper understanding of your progress.

Periodically refine your goals based on reflection. As your understanding of yourself and the game changes, your aspirations may also change. Refining your goals ensures that your pursuits stay in line with your evolving vision of success.

Adopt a continuous improvement mindset. Look at reflection not as a one-time task, but as an ongoing process that's part of your journey. A commitment to continuous improvement can help you stay adaptable and resilient in the ever-changing game.

Think about creating a reflection ritual—a dedicated time and space for introspection. Whether it's a weekly review, a journaling practice, or moments of quiet contemplation, a reflection ritual can be a powerful tool for increasing self-awareness and improving your gameplay.

**Mastering the Game - Tools and Techniques
for Self-Analysis and Improvement**

In the ever-changing game of life, mastering
your performance requires the use of tools and
techniques for self-reflection and improvement.
This chapter introduces a toolbox designed to
help you enhance your gameplay, providing
actionable strategies to evaluate your progress,
refine your strategies, and navigate the complex
and rewarding game of life with intention and
continuous improvement.

1. **Journaling for Self-Reflection:

Take advantage of the power of journaling to
reflect on your journey. Make a habit of writing
down your experiences, thoughts, and emotions.
Journaling gives you a tangible record of your
progress, challenges, and insights, giving you a
comprehensive view of your gameplay.

**2. **SWOT Analysis - Strengths,
Weaknesses, Opportunities, Threats:**

Apply the SWOT analysis framework to assess
your gameplay. Identify your strengths and
weaknesses, opportunities for growth, and
potential threats to your progress. This strategic
analysis allows you to make the most of your
strengths, address weaknesses, and take
advantage of opportunities.

**3. **Goal Setting and Key Performance
Indicators (KPIs):**

Set clear goals and key performance indicators
(KPIs) for your journey. Define specific,
measurable, and achievable objectives.
Regularly measure your progress against these
benchmarks, allowing you to track your
successes and make informed adjustments to
your strategies.

**4. **Feedback Loops - Solicit and Analyze
Feedback:**

Create feedback loops by actively seeking input from trusted sources. Ask for feedback from mentors, peers, and those affected by your actions. Analyze feedback constructively, extracting valuable insights to refine your gameplay and increase your effectiveness.

5. **Data Tracking and Analytics:

Use data tracking and analytics tools to quantify your progress. Whether tracking personal habits, professional milestones, or wellness metrics, data-driven insights provide a quantitative basis for self-analysis. Use this information to make informed decisions and adjustments.

6. **Performance Reviews - Scheduled Self-Assessment:

Include scheduled performance reviews in your gameplay. Set aside dedicated time to assess your accomplishments, challenges, and overall progress. A structured self-assessment allows for intentional reflection and strategic planning for the chapters ahead.

7. **Mindfulness and Meditation Practices:

Incorporate mindfulness and meditation practices to increase self-awareness. These techniques foster a focused and present mindset, allowing you to observe thoughts, emotions, and behaviors objectively. Mindfulness helps you make intentional choices in line with your goals.

8. **Peer Coaching and Accountability Partnerships:

Engage in peer coaching or set up accountability partnerships. Collaborate with people who have similar aspirations. Regular check-ins with peers provide mutual support, encouragement, and opportunities for shared learning and improvement.

9. **Continuous Learning Initiatives:

Commit to continuous learning initiatives. Stay up to date on industry trends, personal development strategies, and new skills relevant to your gameplay. A passion for knowledge enhances your adaptability and prepares you for ongoing improvement.

10. **Visualizations and Goal Boards:

Create visualizations and goal boards to manifest your aspirations. Visualization techniques involve mentally picturing your success, reinforcing a positive mindset. Goal boards serve as tangible reminders of your objectives, keeping your focus sharp and your motivation high.

Crafting Your Personal Toolkit:

Customize this toolkit to fit your unique gameplay style. Try out different tools and techniques, incorporating those that best match your preferences and goals. A personalized toolkit becomes an invaluable resource for mastering the game of life.

Chapter 14: The Endgame - Crafting Your Legacy

In the grand scheme of life, the concept of the endgame encourages us to think about the legacy we want to leave behind. This chapter dives into the profound concept of the endgame, prompting us to contemplate how our journey contributes to a lasting legacy. By examining purpose, contribution, and the reverberations of our influence, we can construct a meaningful narrative that surpasses the complexities of the game.

Defining the Endgame:

The endgame is not just the end of a journey, but a conscious consideration of the legacy we want to create. It involves imagining the effect of our decisions, choices, and contributions on both personal and collective levels. Establishing the endgame provides a compass for intentional living.

Legacy as a Continuum:

View legacy as a continuum—a dynamic thread running through the entirety of our journey. The impact we make today will ripple into the future, influencing generations to come. Think about how our choices align with a legacy that goes beyond immediate accomplishments.

Purpose-driven Contributions:

Constructing our legacy involves aligning our actions with a deeper sense of purpose. What meaningful contributions do we aspire to make? Purpose-driven endeavors fill our journey with profound meaning, forming a legacy that reflects our values and aspirations.

Impact on Others:

Take into account the impact of our actions on others. How do our choices resonate with those around us? The endgame encompasses the

relationships and connections we nurture,
leaving an indelible mark on the hearts and lives
of those who share our journey.

Cultivating a Positive Influence:

Strive to be a positive influence in the lives of
others. Whether through mentorship, support, or
inspiring actions, cultivating a positive influence
amplifies the impact of our legacy. Aim to leave
behind a trail of encouragement, empowerment,
and goodwill.

Transcending Material Achievements:

While material achievements are valuable, the
endgame encourages us to reflect on
contributions that go beyond the material.
Consider how our values, principles, and the
intangible aspects of our journey contribute to a
legacy that resonates on a deeper level.

Environmental and Social Impact:

Expand our gaze beyond personal achievements to consider the environmental and social impact of our legacy. How does our journey contribute to the well-being of the planet and its inhabitants? The endgame involves environmental stewardship and social responsibility.

Documenting Our Journey:

Document our journey for posterity. Whether through writing, multimedia, or other creative expressions, capturing the essence of our experiences preserves the narrative of our legacy. Share our insights, lessons, and the wisdom gained on the path we traversed.

Philanthropy and Giving Back:

Include philanthropy and giving back in our legacy. Actively contribute to causes that align with our values. Philanthropic endeavors become enduring pillars of our legacy, creating a positive impact that extends far beyond our individual journey.

Reflection on a Life Well-Lived:

Envision the reflection on a life well-lived in our endgame. Consider the stories shared, the impact recounted, and the resonance of our legacy. A life well-lived involves not only personal success but the cultivation of a legacy that inspires and uplifts.

Crafting Our Legacy Statement:

Think about crafting a legacy statement—a concise expression of the impact we aspire to make and the values that guide our journey. A legacy statement becomes a guiding light, directing our choices and actions toward the enduring narrative we wish to create.

These remarkable individuals have not only achieved great success in their respective fields, but have also left an indelible mark on humanity through their compassion, advocacy, and contributions to the betterment of society.

Mahatma Gandhi, the leader of the Indian independence movement, not only achieved success in the pursuit of freedom for his nation, but also made a profound global impact with his philosophy of nonviolent resistance, inspiring civil rights movements and leaders around the world.

Mother Teresa, an Albanian-Indian Roman Catholic nun, dedicated her life to serving the poor and sick in Calcutta, India, and her selfless acts of compassion and care for the marginalized made her a symbol of humanitarianism.

Nelson Mandela, a key figure in the anti-apartheid movement in South Africa, not only succeeded in ending institutionalized racial segregation, but also became a global symbol of forgiveness and reconciliation.

Malala Yousafzai, a Pakistani activist for female education, not only survived a Taliban assassination attempt, but continued her advocacy for girls' education worldwide.

 Bill Gates, co-founder of Microsoft, transitioned from a successful career in technology to becoming a prominent philanthropist, focusing on global health, education, and poverty alleviation.

Oprah Winfrey, a media mogul, not only achieved success as a talk show host, actress, and producer, but also made a profound impact on the lives of millions through her messages of empowerment and inspiration.

 Elon Musk, a tech entrepreneur and CEO of companies like Tesla and SpaceX, not only achieved success in revolutionizing the automotive and space industries, but also made a lasting impact on renewable energy and space exploration.

Marie Curie, a pioneering physicist and chemist, not only achieved success with groundbreaking discoveries in the field of radioactivity, but also made a lasting impact on science and medicine.

These individuals have not only achieved remarkable success in their respective fields, but have also left a lasting legacy on humanity. Their stories serve as a reminder that true success is not only measured by personal accomplishments, but also by the positive impact one leaves on the lives of others.

**Chapter 15: Celebrations Along the Journey - Acknowledging Achievements Unlocked

In the exciting game of life, each step forward, every victory, and every milestone is a success to be celebrated—a testament to your strength, hard work, and progress. This chapter emphasizes the importance of recognizing these successes along the way. By acknowledging your accomplishments, you not only cultivate a positive attitude but also bring joy and motivation to the intricate and rewarding game of life.

Fueling Motivation and Momentum:

Acknowledging achievements is a powerful source of motivation and momentum. Recognizing your successes, no matter how big or small, gives you a sense of accomplishment

and pushes you forward with renewed energy.
The momentum gained from celebrating
becomes a driving force for continued progress.

Cultivating a Positive Mindset:

Celebrating successes contributes to the
development of a positive mindset. By focusing
on what you have achieved, you create a mental
landscape that encourages optimism and
resilience. A positive mindset becomes a
foundation for overcoming obstacles and
embracing the game with enthusiasm.

Building Confidence and Self-Efficacy:

Celebrations are essential for building
confidence and self-efficacy. When you
acknowledge and celebrate your achievements,
you reinforce the belief in your ability to
overcome challenges and reach your goals.
Confidence becomes a powerful ally in the
intricate game of life.

Creating Milestone Memories:

Each achievement is a milestone on your journey. Celebrating these milestones creates lasting memories that enrich the fabric of your experiences. These moments of celebration serve as beacons of inspiration, reminding you of your progress and resilience during difficult times.

Fostering a Culture of Gratitude:

Celebrations invite a culture of gratitude. Taking a moment to express gratitude for the successes unlocked, as well as the support and resources that contributed to them, enhances your overall sense of fulfillment. Gratitude becomes a guiding principle in the game of life.

Balancing Ambition with Contentment:

While striving for future goals is essential, celebrating achievements allows you to balance ambition with contentment. Taking time to savor and appreciate the present moment fosters a

holistic perspective on your journey. Balancing
ambition with contentment ensures a more
fulfilling and sustainable game.

Inspiring Others and Building Connections:

Your celebrations inspire others and foster
connections. Sharing your successes with
friends, family, and colleagues creates a ripple
effect of motivation and encouragement.
Celebrations become opportunities to strengthen
relationships and build a supportive network in
the game of life.

Embracing the Joy of the Journey:

Achievements are not just endpoints but integral
parts of the journey. Celebrating them allows
you to embrace the joy inherent in the process of
growth and self-discovery. The joy of the
journey becomes a guiding force, making the
game not only challenging but profoundly
rewarding.

Cultivating a Growth Mindset:

Celebrations align with a growth mindset—a belief that abilities can be developed through dedication and hard work. By acknowledging achievements, you reinforce the idea that challenges are opportunities for learning and growth. A growth mindset propels you forward in the ever-evolving game.

Setting the Tone for Future Success:

Celebrations set the tone for future success. They create a positive cycle of achievement, celebration, and motivation that becomes a self-reinforcing pattern. By celebrating along the way, you pave the road for continued success in the intricate and rewarding game of life.

Create a Celebration Ritual:

Think about creating a celebration ritual—a personal or shared practice that marks achievements along your journey. Whether it's a simple reflection, a symbolic gesture, or a gathering with loved ones, a celebration ritual becomes a meaningful and intentional way to recognize success.

Acknowledging and rewarding personal successes is an essential part of keeping motivation and cultivating a positive attitude in life. Here are some practical tips to help you recognize their accomplishments and take pride in their successes:

1. **Keep a Success Journal:
   - Maintain a success journal to document your successes, big and small. Write down your goals, the steps you took to reach them, and the results. Regularly review your success journal to reflect on your progress and take pride in your journey.

2. **Set Milestone Celebrations:
   - Break down your larger goals into smaller milestones and set specific celebrations for each. Whether it's treating yourself to a favorite meal, taking a day off, or enjoying a small indulgence, setting milestone celebrations provides tangible rewards for your efforts.

3. **Visualize Your Success:

- Use visualization techniques to imagine your success vividly. Picture the moment of accomplishment, the emotions you'll feel, and the impact of your success. Visualization creates a positive mindset and fosters a sense of pride in the journey.

4. **Share Achievements with Others:
- Share your successes with friends, family, or mentors. Let others join in your celebration and recognize your accomplishments. Sharing achievements not only builds connections but also reinforces the significance of your success.

5. **Create a Wall of Achievements:
- Designate a physical or digital space to showcase your achievements visually. Whether it's a bulletin board, a digital folder with certificates and accolades, or a vision board, having a visual representation of your successes serves as a constant reminder of your accomplishments.

6. **Reflect on Personal Growth:

- Take time to reflect on the personal growth and skills developed throughout your journey. Acknowledge how your accomplishments contribute to your overall development. Recognizing the growth achieved along the way enhances your sense of pride.

7. **Reward Yourself Mindfully:
   - Choose rewards that align with your values and contribute positively to your well-being. Whether it's a self-care day, a fitness class, or a hobby you enjoy, select rewards that resonate with your personal aspirations and reflect a healthy and balanced lifestyle.

8. **Express Gratitude for Support:
   - Acknowledge and express gratitude for the support you received from others. Whether it's a mentor, a friend, or a family member, recognizing the contributions of those who supported you enhances the joy of your success and strengthens your relationships.

9. **Create a "Success Playlist":

- Curate a playlist of songs that evoke positive emotions and memories associated with your achievements. Play this "success playlist" during moments of reflection or celebration to enhance the positive atmosphere and celebrate your accomplishments.

10. **Establish a Personal Trademark:
   - Develop a personal trademark or symbol that represents your achievements. It could be a signature gesture, a piece of jewelry, or any item that holds personal significance. This symbol becomes a tangible reminder of your success and a source of pride.

11. **Celebrate Progress, Not Just Perfection:
   - Celebrate incremental progress and improvements, recognizing that success is a journey with continuous growth. Embrace a mindset that values the process and effort invested in reaching your goals, fostering a sense of pride in ongoing achievements.

12. **Host a Success Reflection Ceremony:
   - Periodically host a success reflection
ceremony for yourself. Set aside dedicated time
to review your accomplishments, express
gratitude, and celebrate your journey. Treat it as
a personal ceremony that reinforces the
importance of acknowledging success.

13. **Embrace Positive Affirmations:
   - Incorporate positive affirmations into your
daily routine. Repeat affirmations that reinforce
your achievements, strengths, and capabilities.
Affirmations contribute to a positive mindset
and enhance your sense of pride in your abilities.

Conclusion:

As we come to the end of our journey, it's important to reflect on the lessons we've learned and the insights we've gained. Success is not a static destination, but a dynamic, ever-evolving game. It requires us to view challenges not as roadblocks, but as opportunities for growth. We must surround ourselves with allies who amplify our strengths and persist with resilience in the face of setbacks.

Continuous learning and development are the roots of sustainable success. As we explore uncharted territories and face boss battles, we discover the transformative power of adaptation, the thrill of embracing the unknown, and the strategies required to overcome significant obstacles. The concept of "game over" is debunked, replaced by the perpetual cycle of

reflection, reinvention, and the setting of new
goals.

Crafting a legacy is a poignant contemplation in
the endgame—a legacy not confined to personal
achievements, but one that ripples through the
lives of others, shaping a narrative of purpose,
contribution, and positive influence. Celebrating
achievements, both big and small, fuels
motivation, fosters a positive mindset, and
acknowledges the milestones along this dynamic
adventure.

Success is not a finite state, but a continuous,
never-ending game. It invites us to play with
passion, to learn from every challenge, and to
find joy in the process. It's an adventure where
collaboration, resilience, and the pursuit of
personal fulfillment take center stage.

As you stand on the precipice of your own
narrative, may you carry the lessons of this
journey forward. May you embrace the
uncharted terrain of success with curiosity,

courage, and an unwavering commitment to your personal growth. The game is yours to play, the levels yours to conquer, and the achievements yours to unlock. Here's to the never-ending game—the game of a life well-lived.

THOUGHT:

As we come to the end of our exploration of "Give Up and Lose the Game," let us take a moment to reflect on the realization that life, like success, is an ever-evolving canvas of infinite potential. Our decisions, struggles, and successes all contribute to the unique story of our lives.

The game of success is not confined by strict regulations, but instead is formed by the flexibility of our outlooks, the strength in our souls, and the ongoing quest for growth. In the vastness of our lives, may we find the courage to explore unknown areas, the knowledge to adjust our plans, and the delight in celebrating both minor successes and major accomplishments. As we play the game of success, let us remember that the canvas is not limited by pre-set boundaries; it extends beyond the horizon, encouraging us to dream, create, and redefine success on our own terms.

The journey we take is a symphony of
experiences, a dance of difficulties and successes
that make up the tune of a life well-lived. May
you keep playing, learning, and developing,
understanding that the canvas of your
possibilities is boundless. As you move into the
next chapters of your own story, may the game
be filled with amazement, purpose, and the
unshakable faith that the journey is as wide and
limitless as the horizon itself.

Click For More Interesting books